Track

Also by Norman Finkelstein

Poetry

Inside the Ghost Factory (Marsh Hawk Press, 2010)
Scribe (Dos Madres Press, 2009)
Passing Over (Marsh Hawk Press, 2007)
Powers: Track, Volume 3 (Spuyten Duyvil, 2005)
Columns: Track, Volume 2 (Spuyten Duyvil, 2002)
Track (Spuyten Duyvil, 1999)
Restless Messengers (University of Georgia Press, 1992)

Criticism

On Mount Vision: Forms of the Sacred in Contemporary American Poetry (University of Iowa Press, 2010)

Lyrical Interference: Essays on Poetics (Spuyten Duyvil, 2004)

Not One of Them in Place: Modern Poetry and Jewish American Identity (State University of New York Press, 2001)

The Utopian Moment In Contemporary American Poetry (Bucknell University Press, 1988, 1993)

The Ritual of New Creation: Jewish Tradition and Contemporary Literature (State University of New York Press, 1992)

Norman Finkelstein

Track

Shearsman Books

First published in the United Kingdom in 2012 by
Shearsman Books
50 Westons Hill Drive
Emersons Green
Bristol BS16 7DF

Shearsman Books Ltd Registered Office
30–31 St. James Place, Mangotsfield, Bristol BS16 9JB
(this address not for correspondence)

www.shearsman.com

ISBN 978-1-84861-206-8

Copyright © Norman Finkelstein, 1999, 2002, 2005, 2012.

The right of Norman Finkelstein to be identified as the author of this work has been asserted by him in accordance with the Copyrights, Designs and Patents Act of 1988.
All rights reserved.

Acknowledgements
Track was originally published in three volumes by Spuyten Duyvil, New York: *Track* (1999); *Columns: Track, Volume 2* (2002) *Powers: Track, Volume 3* (2005). We are grateful to Spuyten Duyvil for their permission to reprint this one-volume edition of the poem.
'Statements for *Track*' originally appeared on the website of the Cultural Society, http://www.culturalsociety.org

Contents

I. Forest   7

II. Columns   97

III. Powers   205

Statements for *Track*   303

I
FOREST

for A

(clouds
lightning
feathers
eyes
beasts
tears
kisses)

Revealing traces
Regulating traces
     —Susan Howe

     One steals. One adds numbers.
     He testifies. What
     Is a number past one.
     A number.
               —Jerome Rothenberg

#

TRACK

##

In these operations
no single motif
or portrait

called Emily or K
so long as the letters
arrive to be destroyed.

#

This dying into the work
eliminates all pronouns
the potential for repetition

trace or track
of no event leading
into no depths.

#

This dying into the work
is not for
cannot be mentioned

is stolen
and the prepositions
cannot be mentioned.

#

But for
say you or me
so much for rules

about words or numbers
so much for repetition
in the beckoning depths.

#

So much repetition
in the beckoning depths
it cannot be encompassed

by parts of speech
so that everything connects
or nothing does.

#

As if poetry were epistemology
too smart
for their own good

As if poetry were psychology
too smart
for my own good.

Here I am
said the ghost in the collage
I've been here before

I've been there before
and I wasn't there
said the ghost of the collage.

#

Sightseers should note
the grandeur of the architecture
though much is in ruin

on the road to K
also called Gnosis
in some texts.

#

With a stop along the way
at a haunted house
the lights go on and off

in room after room
as in any
life or narrative.

#

In one room
the light is on forever

Continuity
as interruption

A figure writing
all night long.

#

This was to be
a nursery rhyme
naming the names

which refused to cooperate
and were
and broke his crown.

#

A broken crown
a circle at the center
where the tornado touched down

and hid in the house
couldn't make it to the cellar
with all the names.

##

And so was lost in the forest
among many others
derided or derived

with night coming on
with wolves
with nothing but the Name.

#

Emptied and emptied
at the limit of the zone
you have already traversed

having come to the limit
already
always already.

#

And so broke the promise
to the pronouns among many others
the idle promise

or promise of the ideal
zone or forest
among many others.

#

Wolf son of the Name
the fire in the forest
center of the zone

derided or denied
emptied and emptied
or burning and burning.

#

And in the fire is a face
and in the mirror is a face
and in the mirror is a fire

until the combinations are exhausted
and nothing is left
but a prayer for strength.

#

Blessed are the lines
from one to six
Blessed are the combinations

The thief
and the bride of the thief
and the home among the trees.

##

Call this zone a forest
call this man a thief
call his wife his wife

so that all "falls into place"
And those?
—children of course.

#

Arrived or on the way
one said to another
what is that music?

or no more music
I stole it
said the thief.

#

Falling asleep
afternoon or evening
with no more music

though the house is filled with music
listen wife listen
listen children.

#

Listen to the children
who know their way about the forest
and return with stories

which the thief steals
exchanging them
for a kind of music.

#

Listen to the music
which knows its way about the forest
and returns with stories

which the thief steals
obsessively
thinking they're allegories.

#

Independent as any wife
or thief before his arrest
the stories in the forest

at home in the forest
wait there patiently
to be exchanged for music.

##

In some versions
there is a home among the trees
and in some versions

they live apart
so there are only the letters

In some versions they never meet at all.

#

In some versions
there are many versions
and in some versions only one

around which the commentators
weave endless versions
as if to explain.

#

In these explanations
no single
cause or image

Eden calling
endless promise
endless disaster.

#

Endless promise of disaster
endless disaster of promise

Eden gives way to forest
forest gives way to Eden

In some versions
there is only one version.

#

The collage is the only version
the only version of the forest
in which there is no repetition

but an endless expanse of commentary
Listen carefully
as something disappears.

#

Among the paper trees
a figure glides and stops

Shimmers in a light
that is a sort of music

Turns toward
or away from home.

##

Drunk tonight
in the House of Being

Laughter tonight
in the House of Language

So many
turned away at the door.

#

So many
you would think it a story

an allegory
awaiting commentary

a history
in all its futility.

#

Sew them together
and put them in a drawer

Tell someone
to burn them

Memorize them
and disappear.

#

"All of these indicate that one's self, one's style, one's *persona* exists as such, in its infinitely complex and particular being; that it is not a question of this system or that, but of a total organization which must be described as a self. Style, in short, is the deepest thing in one's being."

#

So that now
all is broken
and has been made whole

So that now
all is whole
and cannot be broken.

#

Thief   House   Forest
Music   Crown   Bride
Allegory   Wolf   Eden
Trees   Letters   Children

I've been there before
I've been here before.

TRACK

##

Letting in all the ghosts
the ghost of the long line
and the ghost of the cascading images

(which she wanted to come back to life)

and the ghost of the king of ghosts
or queen of ghosts
or jack

with whom the numbers are dancing

wishing all the while
for rhapsodic partners.

#

Thus the symmetry
is in the cards:

doubling inappropriate
to the 3 of Waltzes

the 3 of Mirrors

Repressed narcissism

in the poet's mirror
the poet's terror

that it could mean everything
that it could mean at all.

#

A transparent dream
of architecture and landscape

sheaves of wheat
among the looms

in her mother's workshop

Our names in her book

green walls of flowers
and a gift of lace

for my wife who was once a weaver
for myself who has nothing to give.

#

But the poem
the ephemeral
repetitious poem

adorned with some other's
dreams of domes and gardens
workshops and fields

the 19th century
as utopian faith
utopian fate

enfolded in the self.

#

Against symmetry
against repetition
against fatality

but in love with its own fate

it unfolds a set of rules
unfolds as a set of rules
in love with its own fate

which it follows

follows follows

dancing.

##

Another England there I saw
Another London with its Tower

That it has led to this
turning away
captivity
and a Threefold Kiss

Who so wanted the outmost
world   Translucent lovely shining
clear   that I should or should not

fill with woes the passing Wind.

#

As if there were a choice
about Romance
about dreams

Home of the Blessed Dead
Groom With Two Brides

As if there were a choice
about stories

so that you follow the storytellers
inward   mourning your losses
as you mourn the end of a book

#

Which does not end
for all its resemblance
to a life

To live
without plot or fate

But to long
for inevitability

Which does not end
for all its resemblance
to reading a book.

#

But to account for this
numbed vacancy
a formal feeling
stronger than loss
of love or life

would take an explanation
of love and life
extending from birth to death
beginning at any one point
—say now.

#

Goddess of Enactment
at the circumference

Goddess of Trajectory
at every moment

Goddess of Awakening
to the godlessness

Beautiful hollow
core of being

My own being
and the world's.

##

Silence
toward which one goes
crossing desert or sea

of words
by way of words

Silence
as a receding horizon
so that words

crossing desert
or sea.

#

Breaks or confirms
that sense of being

Breaks or confirms
that place

Breaks or confirms
that crossing

Sits still
neither opening nor closing
no longer gesturing

Broken and confirmed.

#

First night
first light
a gift
to the
shammes

An o
pen gift
for you
to re
member.

#

Wants
no memory

Wants
no commentary

Wants
no symmetry

Wants
no poetry

Wants
impossibility.

#

As if
it were coming to an end

So that there are
openings and closings
even while sitting still

Endlessly going back
endlessly going ahead
as if going back

As if (he said)
oh, it is all as if.

##

Proposing fiction
("plot or fate")

Proposing repetition
("I've been here before")

Proposing a space
("put them in a drawer")

Bric-a-brac
in the House of Language

Clues
or souvenirs?

#

She wanted images
postcards from the past
ghosts hovering
above the Irish Sea

stored in the attic

Puppet theater
of exuberance
taken down
from time to time

spoken.

#

This attic
which is desire
which is images

lights blinking
on and off

rhymes
with this damned season

against which
is set
no gestures.

#

Passive voice
absent pronouns
signifying
no desire

signifying desire

Draw a line
leading up from the figure
try
different postures

signifying desire.

#

_____

(the dolls are on the shelf)

_____

(absent gestures)

_____

(the Irish Sea)

_____

(repetition)

_____

(_____)

##

So the house wasn't haunted after all. They packed up and left, pleased with themselves for solving the mystery, having had such a fine time, a real adventure. Bob, after all, had to get back to work, Cindy had lots to do at home, and the kids started school again right after New Year's. The sabotaged car and the cut phone lines, the doors that locked and unlocked on their own, the midnight visit from the Narrative Police—it all made sense now, and they would look back on it and laugh over games of scrabble in the den.

#

A gift to himself
a box of letters
that make words
a box of words
that make numbers

Permission granted
to go on and on
as if among
innumerable
imaginary friends.

#

The spirit of play
as the spirit of structure

Home for the Holidays
Get Out of Jail Free

The collapse of this telegraphy
guarantees its success

Guarantees spirits
between Halloween and Christmas

And on
into the New Year.

#

Master
passing as a friend
passing as the Ghost
of Christmas Past

impossible assimilation

Hellenist
this temple
remains to be purified
waits for the lights

to be numbered.

#

Or an amulet
an antique necklace
swinging
between her breasts

For those
who want images
want numbers
want and want

Permission granted
to go on.

TRACK
(site of the reader)

Walks into death

Room made of books
Made of empty space

Lamp teacup easy chair
Narrative insists on beginning
Insists on ending

After being interrupted
The gestures signify impatience
With purity and with decision
Impunity and inarticulate desire

Qualities arise and shift
Says Our Lady of Parataxis
Weeping in the corner
Abandoned by her knight
On the open plain

Modified by the modifiers
Failing to leap the precipice
The subject is constituted
By a sequence of codes
Lying in bed
Seen by the moon

Proposition or translation
Revision of the second order
A message from the censor
Look there is a message
Behind the mask of another's voice
From Our Lady of the Second Order
Arriving from the seventh moon

Where there is scarcely a drop to drink
The references become romantic
Isolate this statement and count it
Isolate this man and let him
Go through with it and let him
As if climbing a mountain
Wider and wider toward the top
Approaching celestial bodies

Moving too fast the heavens
Music translate this music
Propose this and count it
So that there might be bodies
Material answering material
Jews and Catholics amidst laughter
Perfect clarity of the screen
Perfect clarity of the metonyms
Reading you reading this

One thinks of the decalogue
Power in numbers
Make reference to her mouth and forbid it
Her mouth painted as if it were a text
Her mouth opens as if it were elsewhere
Elsewhere always elsewhere
A crisis uniting cities
Here the lines intersect
Here the lines are parallel
Thou shalt not thou shalt

Wanting to repeat it
Wanting to go down
Not wanting to go down again
Sight of women dancing
The problem of the clerk's desire
Bearing letters or lying
At its feet at her feet
Elusive he or she baring
A matter of preference in fiction

Always leading to disaster
From novel to novel
Sight of letters dancing
A gathering of shards
Look one is slipping away
Look she holds one to her
It's no joke in the sexy cathedral
Longing to enter her book

The overlap becomes intolerable
Threatens to disrupt the numbers
It's no joke say the numbers
We guarantee your accommodations
But only if you stay in bed
Next to her the moonlight
Promises you its power

Enables you to give orders
Entrance of the second person
A crisis of authority
Someone in control here
Behind the mask of the father's voice
Laughed out of the box

Whispers borrowed from the dead
As the box becomes a screen
Viewed by the second person
The message from any moon
Arriving here in the afterlife

Of everything that has been forgotten
The message is given a home
Thank you here is a name
Do not tell it to anyone

Thank you here is a secret
I may or may not have revised
She may or may not be weeping

I wanted to tell you everything
I wanted to change the music

But it fell apart in my hands

TRACK

##

This history
this biography

A frenzy
of interpretation

Suppose
it were to lead elsewhere

No inscriptions
or erasures.

#

Neither telling the truth
nor lying

Staging this road
this hut
this figure with a lantern
in this storm

Either lying
or telling the truth.

#

Suppose
there were only numbers

Magical boundaries
determined or transgressed

Determined and transgressed
here or elsewhere

Here and elsewhere
there were only numbers.

#

Then the figure
(figures)

In this storm
(these storms)

With a lantern
(a lantern)

Lied
(counted).

#

(1) It goes on

(2) You are here

(3) Always arriving

(4) At this stage

(5) The lights are extinguished

(6) Transgressed here and elsewhere

(7)

(8) Lost count.

#

Admired the patience
with which he began again

Begins again
with no care for admiration

With care
for the boundaries

Waits patiently
to begin again.

#

To begin to enter
into being

Always entering
into being

Entering you
entering into being

Entering
this stage.

#

Circling this stage
on which is performed
The Flight of the Numbers
The Flight to the Entrance
after the lights
have been extinguished
and the storm is past
and is going elsewhere.

Left behind
to inhabit the corners

An abandoned machinery
come to life

Which is not life
which creates confusion

Which is not life
no not life at all.

\#

This machinery of confusion
this machinery of interpretation
this storm of interpretation
this storm which has passed

One could ask four questions
one could ask twice over
one could ask of it
over and over.

#

Follows and speaks the name
follows and hears the name spoken

Again and again
the name is spoken

The name
any name

The speaker
any follower.

#

So that the explanations
are cancelled
hover
above the text

In a storm of angels
mighty and dissonant
only any name
becomes one.

#

Dear Angie,
I thought we could spend
some time together
but it is not to be

Disappointed to note
how little this change
really signifies
Love,

#

The Author
(who never turned back
despite his disappointment
never could turn back
because the way was blocked
and the forces arrayed
in such complexity
that he simply

#

Dear J,

It's wrong of you
to put it like that

Wrong of you
to play such games

You could not tolerate
the climate here

Fondly,

#

A

(clouds
lightning
feathers
eyes
beasts
kisses
tears)

broken off

TRACK

recovered

##

Park bench
chess set
gazebo
by water

Any city
anybody
any life
as may be lived.

#

By numbers
by parallel lines
by leaps
forgetting

This move
that significance
any life

Check.

#

—Were there lovers?
　Were there angels?

—There are always birds

—Were there birds in the park?
　Is the figure resting?

—Yes　No

　They are playing a game
　according to instructions.

#

—When will you tell us
　how to move?

—Speak freely despite
　a trace of guilt

—How will we know
　if our moves are correct?

—Speak freely except
　for a trace of guilt.

—When is it over?

—My time is over

—When can we go?

—I leave everything to you

—When can we sleep?

—Do not wake me again

—When can we play again?

—

#

Look there are only three of us
and they are closing in

Look there were eight of us
when they came upon us

Look we are leaderless
and home is far away

It may be the next square
Look there are only two of us.

#

Loitering
around the ruins
by the lake

They took me
into the bad movie

She took me
into that scene

To my lips I set.

#

Called upon
to make sense
to tell a story

No birds

A sheet of flame

Success in failure
failure in success

And this is why.

##

My vocabulary
did this to me

Little Cousins,
Called back

Hagiography
as explanation

Quotation
as dissatisfaction.

#

Programmatic
dissatisfaction:

Bite me
says the apple

Write me
says the body

Yes says the body

No.

#

Put all that behind you
say the instructions
put all this before you

Track as in channel
underground channel
running behind and before

So we have been told
here on the surface.

#

Here where there are trees

Here where there are bodies

Bodies in the marketplace

A message from a dead man

But you sit at your window

Hide among the pages

Hide before the screen

Adjusting the small words.

#

So that these repetitions
become a perpetual farewell

Sentimentality
referring only to itself

Referentiality
sentimentalizing all others

Parallel lines or mimetic doubles

So foul and fair a day I have not seen.

#

Dear J,
The inhabitants of this country

Dear K,
The inhabitants of this letter

Dearest K,
Now that you have moved to the country

Dear T,
You cannot be read as a journal.

#

Resistance to the address
Resistance to the question
Resistance to the instruction
Resistance to the name

In love with memory
In love with closure
In love with repetition
Still in love

#

Still in love
so that there might be
a series of precincts
with gateways between

So that there might be
paths and thresholds
haunted or
holy ground.

TRACK

    ##

Founder or finder
you among the many
traced to the city
you among the lost

You among the last
voices from Paradise
founder founder
whispers the finder.

    #

Whispers of the finder
back before or after
take me   take me
where will you take me

With urgency or agency
lost among the traces
found among the whispers
before or after.

#

Some were fleeing and some were dreaming
some were kneeling and some were sinking
all were together and all were departing
all in all when it started over

All in all started too quickly
spoke too quickly said yes too quickly
as if all could be found
now and at once.

#

Speak quickly of its recurrence
as if this were speech
as if this were recurrence
or something to be found

Were you standing on the wall
falling and falling
were you standing among ruins
falling now and at once?

\#

The ruins were holy
wholly ruins

The fathers came and went
fathers found there

We had come this far
entering the present

Only holy ruins
wholly in the present.

\#

Only in the present
entering the ruins
fathers found there
came and never left

I want to live
here forever
what you have given me
came and never left.

#

How can I say
no farther than this?

Turn my back
on the old resources

Old sources
always at my back

"tiger's leap"
"pile of debris"

#

> Excavation   (Exploration)
>
>   of
>
> Troy   (Chelm)

> Visitors are asked
> not to carry away
> anything they may uncover
> from this site

> Please watch your step

TRACK

What was hung on the walls
to look at

And what was hung on the walls
behind curtains or screens

What was framed
and what was left unframed

And what was left behind.

Became a romance
of the ruins

Low stone wall
always figured

Figures on the wall
reading or to be read

Or reading one another.

#

Call this the first picture
passed on or down

Pass on or down
and the atmosphere changes

Lightens or darkens
in comedy or tragedy

Pass up or down.

#

Call this the second picture
and stop counting stop looking

They are all behind a screen
extending from anywhere
to before and after

This is not a gallery
and not an excavation.

#

Neither tourist nor pilgrim
nor aficionado

Neither I nor you
nor any third person

Neither the path before
nor the path after

And god forbid any pictures.

#

Of the discontinuity:
prevention of pictures

Of the formation of pictures:
continuously

Of monumentality:
calling for illustration

Forever denied.

#

"to the seventh year
beyond the seventh year
of the seventh year"

Last seen buried
beneath a monument of prose
composing the last picture

As per instructions.

##

Pure luck
(like rolling sevens)

Having nothing to do
with following instructions

Seven years
and the unlucky ones

Need a sabbatical.

#

And the seven lean ones
ate up the seven fat ones

As is usually the case

This came in a dream

As is usually the case

Hungry cattle
playing with loaded dice.

#

I wracked my brain

> *Those were the instructions*

I kept rolling sevens

> *Those were the instructions*

I ate up all the cattle

> *The fat ones and the lean ones*

I dreamed I ate all the instructions.

#

And at the moment of crisis
all the combinations
all the coincidences
take on a spooky radiance

called the bright light of shipwreck
called the gentle flame of his story
strong light of the canonical.

#

Which we would undermine
however the lights
may form new constellations

Which we may observe
night after night
a lesson from the universe

Which we repeat.

#

    Monday
    Tuesday
    Wednesday
    Thursday
    Friday
    Saturday
    Sunday.

#

    Wednesday
    Wednesday
    Wednesday
    Wednesday
    Wednesday
    Wednesday
    Thursday.

Sometimes there are numbers
and sometimes there are ruptures

Sometimes the rules
break the continuities

And sometimes the continuities
break the rules

Sometimes a seventh is added much later.

#

This is coming much later
and only for its own sake

This is coming in the fall
when it has come before

This is falling like leaves
from the tree of heaven

Which fell for its own sake.

Found somewhere between
Magic and possibility
Like a number or metaphor

On the border of the real

Like a number or metaphor
Magic and possibility
Found somewhere between.

#

Like her mirrors on the page

Her page of mirrors

On the border of sense

Reflection of the fallen

Tree of heaven

Reflection of the fallen

Fallen world of repetition.

#

And in this
and in this

And in this
and in that

What did she see?
what did she reflect?

Page after page.

#

Say the lost mother
is Lady Luck
who scatters words at random
page after page

Say that she takes
the young boys at random
page after page.

#

Say you came to that world
and were permitted to stay

The tree of heaven
a mirror of stars

Say you were a page
as luck would have it

What would you say?

(Collage II)

I was serving wine
out on the verandah

A bird flew by
with a ring in its beak

That matched the ring
that my mistress wore

Seven stones in a ring upon her right hand.

       #

The ring fell into the cup
the cup fell to the floor
the wine flowed from the cup
and flooded the stone floor

The bird laughed in the tree
that stretched from earth to heaven

Seven birds in seven branches of a tree with seven roots.

#

My mistress lies in a pool
Wine or blood or the green salt sea

My mistress floats or drowns
Say the words to take us away

My mistress sleeps in the house
Nothing can save us from song

And there is nothing to see in the pool.

#

    Lately I have dreamed
    of too many women
    living and dead

    Oh turn me turn me

    Lately I have dreamed
    too many dreams
    asleep or awake.

#

Lately I've written
too few letters—

Dear R why
this fatal stasis?

Why these medieval
trappings why

these strange intersections?

#

I who was once a page
asleep beneath a tree

I who was once a bird
who stole a ring that was her heart

I who was once a lady
with a ring around her heart

write to you from the world.

#

Write to the world
silly poems of neglect
sly seductive notes

So many I've stopped counting
here among the numbers
here where I stop counting

At the center of the world.

##

And so took his leave
took the leaves strewn
around his room

Found when he awoke
waiting to be gathered
into a sentence

Speaking of fate.

#

Speaking of his fate
but why now?

Speaking of his return
did he ever return?

I think he comes and goes
can you count on it?

Did he ever leave?

#

He left forever
only to return
as the ghost of answering questions

Ghosts return
only when the fullness
is passing from the year

The fullness of years passing from his fate.

#

So the fullness passes
from the soul of the flesh

Flesh of the soul
drawing closer and closer

Passing away
or drawing closer

The sentence of the soul in the flesh.

#

Nothing like wisdom
in its coming and going

Nothing fleshly
in the sentence of its fate

Something soulful
as the flesh draws closer

Closer and closer draws his fate.

#

But end on a couplet
of sentence and soul

Writing the Absolute
coming to the bride-self

Write the material

Say two people
are in love.

#

Say in this sentence
two people are in love

Say love comes quietly
at the end of the sentence

which has no ending

This bed thy center is,
these walls thy sphere.

##

"In old age/the mind/
casts off/rebelliously"

Mid-life the mind
grows more aware
of its boundaries

Called fate or chance
—the eagle on its crag.

#

So that love defines a boundary
beyond which he will not go

The center is everywhere
and the circumference nowhere

So that in the space evacuated
by a retreating deity

Two lovers embrace.

#

And then come apart?

Try calling this
catastrophe creation

Condition of fire
toward which we wander out of bounds

Love is not love, etc.

#

Dear M the bark
in the sonnet and the painting
and your poem about the painting

Are they on course or wandering
with limbs intertwined?

Has fate brought them here
with eyes wide open?

#

And if the water "they" cross
is infinitely dark

Dear N I am sorry
I have not answered your letter

Dear Barnabas I am sorry
you will not be rescued

O my friends.

#

Under the sign of Mercury
messages come and go

Borne through the air
and across the water

Born under the sign
that comes and goes

I say yes and no to my fate.

#

Instead of a letter
a letter

Instead of a poem
a poem

Instead of seven
six

And one.

##

<u>One</u>

M. Mallarmé
throws his dice

Chance launching us
into the abyss

Such is our fate
amidst wave and flame.

#

<u>Two</u>

In flames
or waves of passion

Passing through figures
as in Bergman's film

Bound together
by the music of the flute.

#

Three

Ladies seen
by two poets

Robert and Robert
speaking about love

In all its fatality
singing about love.

#

Four

In a garden
in a discourse in a garden

The sages speak
from a condition of freedom

Conditional freedom
in a paradise of speech.

<u>Five</u>

Out of seven
days of labor

Unending labor
in a single moment

Unending motion
even at rest.

#

<u>Six</u>

After which
comes rest

That it is good
as it is to be

But how
is it to be?

#

<u>Seven</u>

at rest

a chance

at rest

to accept

how it is

to be.

TRACK

##

On this day he threw coins
and on this day he threw wands

Pearwood inlaid with silver
seeking a number.

#

Sought pearwood inlaid with silver
to be played in the Room of the Peacocks
with silver coins at their feet

Say four.

#

A kind of beauty
after a kind of horror

A history of affect
that we carry with us.

#

A kind of beauty
that is a kind of horror

Down the museum corridors
a kind of truth.

##

Not beauty but strangeness
will become the other

Not beauty but strangeness
will win out over time.

#

Not beauty but strangeness
in the Room of the Peacocks

The strangeness of the other
down the corridors of time.

#

"And truth? O,
Truth!"

If you say so,
old man.

#

Truth in the corridors
corridors of horror

The old men crowded there
and the children.

##

Kept in line
as a kind of contrivance

Kept in line
by the old men.

#

Kept alive
with the old men and the children

In the contrived corridors
the cunning passages.

#

Encrypted
scratched on the walls

*Ganz und gar nicht
hermetisch.*

#

Sealed, ensouled
bearing within

Encircled seed
burning within.

On this day all was thrown
and on this day all was written
and on this day all was repeated

And so on.

But on this day all
may be lifted up
may be cast off
may be unsealed.

Maybe this has gone
as far as it may go

Maybe this soul has gone
and will never return.

Maybe the old
will return as children

Cast off

Cast off   cast off.

II
COLUMNS

Verbracht ins
Gelände
mit der untrüglichen Spur:
             —Paul Celan

TRACK

##

Now Duncan goes up
into that great constellation

Love in his hands
like a newborn star

Like a track across the sky
the lights lit in order

Across a sea of numbers
an uncountable host.

#

In the immeasurable world
suspended in emptiness

Suspended voices
in the loft above

What is to be met with
resting on air?

What is to be discerned
in this sudden sound?

#

A rift in the world
or world of the rift

World of combinations
world of orders

Spoke to the world
because of the world

Spoke or sang
to or of the world.

#

If it is an order
if it falls into line

If for any reason
a world lost

Or if it goes on
turns and goes on

"Preise dem Engel die Welt"
—even so.

הנני׳
an answer

That is a question
to be answered

An answer
that is a place

Or our answer
that is not a place.

#

"He is the place of the world
but the world is not his place"

Walking into a picture
"fraught with background"

Three days walking
out of myth into history

Endlessly walking
into the history of our response.

#

Responded to the children
for the sake of the children

Would sacrifice this child
for sake of the children

Would walk across the desert
of or into history

Writing history
for the sake of the children.

#

But to profane
this sacred history

But to sacrifice
this deserted writing

To call and call
knowing he will answer

To answer
not knowing if he calls.

##

Easy enough
to set the scene

Find the
circumstances

Space
which may be filled

Silence
which may be broken.

#

Or was that
"spoken"?

What is
"heard" here?

What are
"the circumstances"?

Don't ask questions
someone once said.

#

Said that
long ago

In the course of a life
now over

Yet I "hear" him
I "answer"

Could give you
his name.

#

You taking notes
take note of this:

He and I
are here together

Neither of us
need to be named

It is a subject to be addressed
to be "taken up."

##

Speaking to the dead
for the dead

Speaking of speaking
to or for the dead

Speaking what was
whispered in secret

Speaking the whispers
of or in the clouds.

#

Whispered writhe
or wraith

Whispered writhing
wraith words

Writhing wraiths
whispered the word

Writing wraiths
whispered beauty.

#

The whispers rise
into the clouds.

The wraiths rise
into the beautiful writing

The wraiths writhe
when beautifully written

The wrathful writing
rises and writhes.

#

The dead remain dead
self-possessed, self-contained

Or possessing others
however self-contained

Dybbuks and cloud-Jews
keeping their distance

So as to say
goodbye to ourselves.

TRACK

##

You see him strolling
along West End Avenue
briefcase in hand

And you say goodbye
because he never existed
except in possibility.

#

You say goodbye
to him among others
in senseless repetition

Formula of recuperation
after endless losses
limited possibilities.

#

Dwindling to a point
in some fashionable neighborhood
where you are only a visitor

And the background shifts
and they keep on talking
as you leave the room.

#

It is almost a story
but let's sit this one out
almost on a dare

Dare him to become
any possibility
found in your file.

#

There in his briefcase
your file in his briefcase
his file in yours

Not strolling but hurrying
a courier among couriers
possessed of secrets.

#

Going from room to room
hardly speaking
with a briefcase full of files

Almost on a dare
he considers the possibilities
—sits this one out.

##

Shed like a skin
he becomes his absence
and so is always there

And you take up residence
in the shape of his absence
and so

#

Recognize
your face in the mirror
recognize yourself

Strolling in the distance
someone else
as he disappears.

#

More or less than game
more or less than confession
neither psyche nor episteme

Rather a tune
sung out of nowhere
before it disappears.

#

"So that"—
the consequences
of such an act

Signify
what is really a movement
going from here to there.

#

"So that"
he returns to wandering
a theme like any other

Nomadic variations
conducted in the wilderness
in the presence of presence.

#

Unquestionably a psyche
unquestionably an episteme
unquestionably more

Or less—
say a song
say an invention.

##

Say an opening
as in a game

An opening
in the middle of things

"Reb Derasha
opened."

#

That was one way to do it
and this is another

Why is it this way
and not another?

Why this game?

Why a game at all?

#

These discontinuities
mark a passage
—of this rest assured

And rest assured
that the game is serious
—which is why we play.

#

Now the game played
in this tractate

Now the subject addressed
in this section

Now the
in this

#

In this
now the the
a third time

The other two
are gone

Now.

#

It leads to up to this:
goodbye, dear friend

Now you are part
of the inscriptions

Now you
have done your part.

##

Afterwards
an aftertime
an afterword

A shuttling
between fiction and history
a balance.

#

Afterwards
an antitime

Unbalanced slide
hour of lead

Fiction and history
in a single stroke.

#

Gone
in a single stroke
gone into the world

Or gone
into that world
leaving me.

#

Empty house
empty landscape

Evacuated
of all meaning

Save this

Save this.

#

Save this remnant
these scraps of meaning

"Or else remove me hence
unto that hill"

Or else

Or else.

#

After the fall
the wind blows
the river flows
over the fall

A refrain:
sing again!

##

It is to be regarded
as three melodies
made of the same notes

Or three views
of one sculpture
in a single space.

#

It is to be regarded
as one frame
with two sides
in three dimensions

It is to be regarded
as perfectly complete.

#

1+2+3
1x2x3

Which proves
the need for rhetoric

Which proves
the need for song.

#

Upper limit
music of the spheres

"what he had in mind
was planetary"

What was planetary
was his mind.

#

Lower limit
speech

Yet "It is unspeakable,
that which exists."

To say
that.

#

The perfection
of the unspeakable

The unspeakably perfect

##

I have always wanted to test
the limits of the poem;
I have never been satisfied

dwelling within its boundaries.
I came to this work
in quiet desperation,

#

placing my faith in a hard-won,
still faulty
knowledge of measure.

I knew I had to set the rules
and break them. I knew
my work would be hard to conceive.

#

From the start I knew
that I would have to cross the boundary
of the line, that the sudden excesses,

the terrible diminutions,
might be impossible to bear.
Perhaps I was wrong

#

to think of the poem as anything
but a vessel—to hold thought still
but moving in place.

There was something to say
and there was nothing to say,
there was a bustling practice

#

and there was a sudden drop.
What was there
to count on ?

Nothing, really.
But I went on anyway
taking the measure if nothing else.

#

I wanted an author
and I wanted an interlocutor

When no one,
nothing was sufficient,

I wanted a friend
to say enough.

TRACK

##

Born against the time
born with a caul
not born but found
a foundling among foundlings

Later cast spells.

#

Later told stories
of cauls and spells
cast against history

Later histories told
of calls and spells.

#

Later histories found
these stories inadequate
to the call of their spell

Later histories were found
to be inadequate.

#

The earliest histories
were found in books
buried in a chest
protected by spells

Cast by a foundling.

#

The earliest histories
(proven accurate)
told of a foundling
buried in a chest
among books of spells.

##

The degree of ritual
corresponds
to the scatter
the risk

Found there.

#

They went up the mountain
playing mandolins and pipes
the deep notes echoing
across the valley

All but one.

#

All but one
among the unfinished
the sports and bunglers
fleeing the judgment

The spell of the family.

#

The bee keeper
the bear trainer
"the toupee artiste"
and the helpful sentry—

All the righteous ones—

#

Magically escaped

In a contrivance
a contraption
something with wheels

And wings.

○ ✡

"With these two signs the Israelites and the necromantic Jews have done much and brought about much. They are still kept highly secret by a number of them. For these two have such a strong power that everything that can be done by characters and words is possible for these two."

#

Also regarded
as unruly, rebellious
"naughty" like Eros
that stirs up

The well-ordered cosmos.

#

Yet sometimes associated
with marriage
combining the masculine 3
and the feminine 2

For purely mathematical reasons.

#

A blessing
a curse

Talisman
or outstretched hand

Expressed with a different word.

#

Lovers' knot
upon a shield
carried from the East

Into the green wood
on such a day.

##

This was intended
to be a book of magic

Forbidden spells
written and unwritten

Cast in time.

#

This was intended
to be cast against time

So that the spells
would be unwritten

At the moment he enters.

#

This has been cast
as the controlling moment

For better or worse

Better and worse
as time goes on.

#

Like the laughter of children
over a field of graves

Like almond trees upon a hillside

Rosemary for remembrance
woven in a wreath.

#

A commandment woven
into the fabric of their lives

Power greater
than any spell

Any intention.

##

What power broods
over the image-trove

Forbids us to summon
the wealth of creation

Keeps us listening?

\#

Keeps us bound
to the memory of our freedom

Keeps our freedom
beyond any image

Keeps creation bound?

\#

Or unbound?

"If the abysm /
Could vomit forth its secrets . . .
But a voice / Is wanting,
the deep truth is imageless."

#

Voiceless
imageless
absence
upon absence

Or absence of absence.

#

Lost father
to lost father:

Loss
to loss:

הנני'

TRACK

(Chai)

One is a book of music
One is a spire
One is an alphabet read backwards
One is a bridge into the void
One is a bridge
One is the void
One is a glyph that stands for void
One is a translator
One is a translation
One is a star hidden in a translation
One is a star revealed to a philosopher
One is a star seen in the countenance
One is the radiance of that star
One is all that disappears in that radiance
One is a leap into darkness
One can fend for itself
One is a thief
One is not a number

TRACK

		IS IT NOT IT IS

Older than the world
and apart from it.

Younger than the next moment
the next moment.

Fold after fold
one comes to her
fold after fold.

Fold after fold
one comes to her
fold.

Fold after fold
one comes
to rest.

##

It is a history of random events
left out by accident

Left out by accident?

No repetitions are permitted.

#

It is a history of random events
which constitute a life

So that nothing
may be repeated.

#

Why acquiesce
to all that is demanded?

Why demand
that all acquiesce?

#

It is a history
of demands and acquiescence

A history of repetitions
which constitute a life.

##

Expands exponentially
without a subject

All are subject
to this expansion

Of the heart.

#

That simple?

Must be
to be recognized

Must be recognized
as that simple.

#

They meant eye to eye

Looks out

Leaps up

They meant the heart
to be the subject.

#

The heart is the subject
expanding exponentially
with each passing year

It's that simple
my love.

#

"Not in the heavens . . .
Not across the sea . . .
Rather, near to you is the word, exceedingly,
In your mouth and in your heart,
To observe it!"

(*Twice Chai*)

These lines
would form a triangle

These triangles
would form a star

This star
is light.

#

This is the hidden one
unheard and unseen

Forever delayed
beyond the horizon

Suddenly manifest
calling and calling.

#

The Baal Shem Tov
The Maggid of Meseritz
Rabbi Moshe Leib of Sassov
Rabbi Israel of Rishin

—at which point
it becomes a story.

\#

He sat in his castle
on his golden chair.

He sat on a stool
in a corner by the fire

And we can tell the story
of how it was done.

\#

We can tell the story
of the fire and the star

We can return to the place
and say the prayer

We can pray or forget
or pray to forget

\#

Or forget to pray?

These lines would form
These triangles would form
This star would hover
Unheard
and unseen.

(Collage III)

Museum of antiquities
collection of curiosities
catalogue of rarities
plunder of centuries

All that was created
in seven days
gathered and displayed.

#

An ape of agate
a jade grasshopper
three hundred golden bees
a precious stone from a vulture's head
silver buckles, iron pins, copper plates

and a brass jew's harp that last sounded
on the crossing over the black water.

#

Accompanied by gourd rattles
conch shells
ram's horns
and muffled drums

Played by hooded figures
of gods or men

On a lifeless ocean.

#

As luck would have it
There was a story to tell
A birth or a death

A journey to the center

A birth or a death
There was a story to tell
As luck would have it.

#

Sister to sister
in a leafy grove
shadowed by figures
or figured in shadows

Shallow talk
over dismembered bodies
Dog head he was fed

#

before the tale began.

The lovers went walking
under starlight or moonlight
phase after phase
upon a great wheel

But this is no wheel

This is a path.

#

This is the way
and the search for the way

The route leads
from the forest to the book

Sojourners in time
arriving in time

Rest.

##

Twos and fours, he read
auspicious
good luck solidifies
built into blocks
strong, rhythmic
doubly foundational
angles defined
cleanly broken.

\#

By twos and fours, he read
propaedeutic
as if in school
he took the measure
as he had been instructed
back to another
instructed before him
in the workings thereof.

\#

That among these numbers
rhapsodic
heights, depths
scaled, plumbed
ancient of days
with instruments
across distances
across the void.

#

That among these repetitions
disjunctive
try as one might
say cleave
say syntax
say again
again
unresolved.

#

These resolutions may lead us
arbitrary
gathered on a hillside
gathered on the shore
waiting then scattered
counting ourselves lucky
in an abstract discourse
in which we cannot be seen.

#

Take heart my dear ones
beneficent
that I come to you
that I turn away
given then taken
promise
make a list
granted.

#

Flowering late and dark
romantic
dreams and threats
rings, lockets
locks of hair
knuckle bones, ash
borne on the wind
born as music.

#

Each object, each path
hermeneutic
found between the realms
a hermetic order
of everyone and no one
dressed in masks
and outlandish costumes
we wear everyday.

##

Thrice threefold the gates
ninefold in strength
remaining to be opened

By a perilous key
to work the machinery
to work our woe

Three folds were brass,
three iron,
three of adamantine rock.

#

Until a bridge is built
a way is paved
across Chaos

Three several ways
in sight to each
of these three places led

So each of us
may go to Hell
in his own fashion.

#

Or three sinners
in three mouths
told in threes

And who would climb
those shaggy flanks—
reverse themselves

At the nadir
*conviensi dipartir
da tanto male.*

#

But hell now
is not exterior
is not to be got out of

Who knew
that obscurity
all too well

Yet rose
to great heights
in that world.

#

Meaning this world
where we
may gather hellflowers

Meaning this world
where hellflowers
still bloom

A few scattered
among plainer blooms
come what may.

#

Come May
lost daughter
lost sister

Lost time
never having left
that other world

Remains here
in limbo
with flowers in her hair.

#

It is only
in the imagination
(I once said)

So that hell
and heaven
are a kind of potential

The imagination
a kind of potential
a kind of love.

#

He would say
folding his hands
as if saying amen

Having known hell too
go ahead
well done

Since he too
taught me
to count.

#

Thrice threefold
I have counted
come what may

Perhaps my only
way out of hell
counting in threes

The number orange
the number Mars
the number spell.

##

Strange to think
that by spells and numbers
quotations, repetitions
endless reflection

A sufficient pattern
should or should not emerge

Strange reflection
that by endless spells
quotations, repetitions
numbers think.

#

A pattern emerges
sufficient unto the day

A language pattern
that can or cannot be

A pattern language
carried along the way

A way of carrying
language along the way

Sufficient to carry one
on the way to language.

#

Paradise the accommodation
of violent incursions
repeated impediments
along the way

Paradise the inoculation
of verbal shocks
measured sequences
of a larger pattern

Paradise the pattern

Paradise the way.

#

Paradise no telos
but part of a larger pattern
one dream among many
at any one time

Landscape or figure
painted over and over
the world becoming
the museum of itself

Renewed by each viewer
visiting the world.

\#

Not tourists but pilgrims
not sights but shrines

Paradise the way
—way of the world

Broad or narrow
always a risk

Always at risk
of falling away

Shrine to chaos

Museum of nothingness.

\#

In the museum of nothingness
the empty frames
the solitary pedestals

In the museum of paradise
the ultimate elegance
the imagined land

Withdrawn once again
withdrawn into itself
—clouds upon the mountain

No message from the throne.

#

Came upon the combination
unlocked the words

Numbers unlocked
the words that waited

Numbers unlocked
the words that were numbers

The words that were numbered
combinations, repetitions

Numberless
words.

#

I mean in the streets
and what pass for cafés

and what the cafés passed for
in anticipation or regret

At that point
(meaning this point)

I mean the antics
the mimes and puppets

I mean the antiques
in anticipation and regret.

#

I mean paradise
mistaken for the metropole
(and vice versa)
by the children of paradise

The exiles from paradise
in the streets they've been denied.
—or "glassed in dreams"
the walls become mirrors

That they see themselves
as they are or might become.

#

Paradise the suspicion
of affirmation

Or affirmation of suspicion
insufferable elegance

Elegance to be resisted

Resistance made elegant

In what remains to me here
would bring as much beauty
as the poem can bear

Gazing upon the pillars of the world.

Intermezzo

COLUMNS
(Arithmetical Ruins)

Always
the villages
in the background

Roosters
with women's heads
cows

Carrying torahs
as they have
been given

As if
there were nothing
but Jews!

#

Pillars
of fire
of flowers

An iconography
complete
as the crowds

No judgment
is final
saith the king

His vertical harp
the lovers
horizontal.

#

Jerusalem
Jerusalem
an exile

Heading
toward the chupah
the elongated bride

Shofar
and candelabrum
on wings

Naked
among trees
beneath the crown.

○

Inspired
the prophet
encircles himself

Green beard
green Jew
the book the tablets

The tallis
across the loins
here

Is a cross
here
it is gone.

(for A)

Your colors
Tristesse
could live
among the parakeets

Angular
in a
rounded
world

Your angles
Tristesse
could calm
the conflagrations

Swirling
among
the tan
newspapers.

#

These windows
are not
windows (yellow
mimosa)

This woman
bathing
these pink
towels

These men
in the office
this man
in the mirror

Are not
these colors
riche
très riche.

#

This table
is a landscape
this house
is a landscape

These forms
are a house
(by a canal)
(inside out)

These lines
are called a forest
night
thrown and thrown

A different canal
a different house
the same story
the same ending.

##

Capricorn
rules the mermaids
among receding
landscapes

Capricorn
triumphant
the unconscious
become technique

Technique
master
a chimera
at the café

Abused
the word
walking by
so wounded.

#

And so to follow
his unmistakable track
driven into the terrain
that is the world

It cannot be—
it need not be—
still
the same urgency

How every stroke
could prove a revelation
could prove insufficient
at every turn

No abstraction
before such memories
no dreamwork
could ever suffice.

#

So that the exchange rate
image hoard to word hoard
is rendered null
and void

Plaster clouds
upon a painted ceiling
the promise of eternity
broken when made

Better to cut
an agreement in the flesh
which perishes
though the agreement remains

Remains or returns—
הנני
—I still seem
to be here.

##

Unwilling traveler
you come back to summer
reminder of death
the verdant lover
or never the lover
never the reader
transformed by the book.

Back to no luck
to chance the trickster
mask of the self-willed
autodidact
facing his ignorance
and learning too late
or never learning.

As a boy you read
the price of fate
and plucked out an eye
to become a god
on an eight-legged steed
thought and memory
the birds on your shoulders.

Now what you believe
languishes unread
indecipherable
in stultifying heat
crowded masses of paper
canvas raft that is your life
drifting away.

I came back from Paris
because I was you
standing before the graves
in Montparnasse
each grave was the same
told the same story
ended the same way.

Years and years
field stone, snow stone
blood spilled
on snow and stone
white flowers reenacting snow
petals falling upon stone floors
washed forever in blood.

Now and forever
Heureuse your caress
Tristesse your inspiration
breath in the ear
like the order of music
or the scent of her hair
as the measure of love.

Impossible the stone
as the fingers press
into the flesh of the thigh

Impossible the metamorphoses
stories of changes
changing to stone

Com-
plications of perfection
(compli-

Cations of rhythm)—
this girl
this tree.

#

So there was
music
since there was dancing

Since there was mystery
standing before the painting
falling into place

"Nor was
La Calunnia
painted"

That music
and now
this.

#

Not the descent of a god
nor the summons from above
but the simple entrance

Round a corner
or into a room
—there

It was—
almost weeping
for the pleasure of it

"The rest of Life to see!"
—call this my
Parable of the Blind.

#

Naked in the allegory
Truth like Love
draws our sight

And in those stanzas
most beautiful of puns
we cast our gaze

Cast like a boy
with a helmet and sword
arch and girlish

Taking pleasure in that power
handed over to love
naked in the truth.

TRACK

##

Came out from among
giants
heading
toward giants?

We were in our eyes
like grasshoppers
and thus were we
in their eyes!

Came out from among
the pillars of the world
intact but in ruin
perfect world of ruins

So that what was behind
was what lay before—
Yehoshua son of Nun
and Calev son of Yefunne:

The land that we crossed through,
to scout it out—
good is that land
exceedingly, exceedingly!

#

Neither the Tuscan hills
nor the Wadi of Clusters
old and older
worlds from which you've come

Neither the Vernaccia
of San Gimignano
nor the syrupy purple
of the Passover seder

From a clear spring
at the base of what hill?
what middle flight?
what adventurous song?

Veering and veering
Discontinuity
abides and constitutes
herself as Presence

Break me
be with me
forty days
forty years.

##

Or is life itself
that intermezzo
as much behind you
as before?

Music the wilderness
in which you wandered
sweetly dissonant
moments, notes

The years as catches
read so long ago
"an iron bell of joy"
sounding in the deep

So that the passage of time
grows perceptible
here among the passages
of notes or text

Saving liberty from nothingness
restoring our freedom
as we acknowledge the Law
that saved us from bondage.

#

Saved us from what
or for what
again and again—
can't help but ask

Erev Rosh Hashanah
5761
you taking notes
take note of this

An aging Jew
in exile from exile
away at home
attends upon the almond tree:

*Diaspora
is still the way
of shreds and shards,
of all that frays,*

*discolored words,
and leaves astray,
and winds that scatter
nesting birds—*

##

As if no words
could ever be my own

As if each word
stands in for another

These have been the fears
the enabling fears

The motives for spying
upon the lands of others

Possession and disinheritance
stalking the word

Haunting the word land—
𝔎𝔢𝔫𝔫𝔰𝔱 𝔡𝔲 𝔡𝔞𝔰 𝔏𝔞𝔫𝔡…

Oh I do
but I left long ago

Now I am returning
forever returning

Lemons and oranges
milk and honey

Wandering in the passage
between the words and the things.

#

with mighty wings outspread

Out of our evil seek to bring forth good

with difficulty and labour hard

feed on thoughts that voluntary move

Sufficient to have stood, though free to fall

Their starry dance in numbers that compute

wounds of deadly hate

with many a rill

With mazy error under pendent shades

into their inmost bower

Love unlibidinous reigned

self-begot, self-raised

my sect thou seest

sulphurous and nitrous

The grassy clods now calved

What next I bring shall please thee

death is to me as life

And for thee, whose perfection far excelled

See, Father, what firstfruits on Earth are sprung

add love

(in memory of Ronald Johnson)

##

Forty years in the desert of meaning
lost opportunities strangely contrived

Forty days in the deluge of meaning
two by two as previously arranged

Forty signs expecting completion
miscomputed or misconstrued

Forty lines suddenly recovered
meaning they were here all along

Meaning was here all along
wilderness or flood

Or flooded wilderness
evacuated of meaning

Jarring of place
place of the jar

In which nothing could be lost
so that nothing would be lost

Except except
stones from a mountain

Meaning this
and this

#

Dear T,

I think I understand what Spicer means in his first letter to Lorca when he writes that the letters "will establish the bulk, the wastage." He declares that "they are to be as temporary as our poetry is to be permanent"; that in the letters, "We will use up our rhetoric . . . so that it will not appear in our poems." He calls the letters "unnecessary," though they are written, it seems, to leach out some sort of verbal dross—which would make them very necessary indeed. And of course, they appear in the midst of the poems, and have had at least as much influence. Spicer must have understood this by the time he includes the letter to Blaser in *Admonitions*: after all, he tells Blaser that "This is the most important letter that you have ever received."

When I realized that I had miscounted in this movement, that I had written 3x20 lines instead of 4x20, I experienced a moment of sheer panic, despite what I've written about disasters, discontinuities, verbal shocks, and that which we "loveth best" revealing itself only against or through the structure. Hence this letter, which is absolutely necessary, in the same way it was deemed necessary for the Hebrews to wander in the desert for forty years after almost entering the Promised Land. I haven't been wandering in the desert of meaning for forty years, but I have been here long enough to understand that the temporary can become permanent in all sorts of surprising ways. That's just as well: the Promised Land is only a horizon; its promise ceases the moment one enters.

Thanks again for your continued support—and patience.

Love always,

N.

TRACK

##

Always
at a certain point
there comes an address:

"Be patient that I address you in a poem,
        there is no other
                fit medium."

No other place
where patience and desire
may meet.

#

Place and medium
destination and way
relaxed yet urgent

Acknowledgment:
another
to whom one speaks

And there is an answer
even in silence
there is an answer.

#

Which is to say
it answers itself

Which is an answer
that is not an answer

Which is to say
there is no answer

That is not itself
a repetition

Of a repetition.

But above all
an art
of generous proportions

Expansive
hospitable
but measured withal

Housed in
and housing
a world.

#

And are we passing
at last into anagogy?

City and garden
quest and marriage

The forms of nature
in an infinite mind?

Imaginative limit
of our desire

Housing the body of the world.

#

Seen in the sky
or observed in the eye

Infinite desire
blessed over and over

He bid me return
come back again soon

As in the dream long before
he and my father

When I had to go.

##

Seeking to fasten
upon an object of mourning
to be saved from melancholy

The shadow of the object
fell upon the ego
henceforth to be judged

By a special agency
as though it were an object
the forsaken object.

#

Seeking to flee
from the loss of the other
the loss of the self

Came upon
an expansive fantasy
innumerably numbered

Within and without:
Ezekiel's fractals
alight in Oz.

#

Led there by music
neither the self's nor another's

Music from nowhere
heard on the wind

Coming by ship
by thrones in the sky

Freed from the wreckage
freed by the wreckage

You were there too.

TRACK

##

Reread your life
like a belovèd book
but filled with ambivalences
and of dubious authorship

Reread the book—
any book you have loved—
of antique matter
and strange devices

In this new setting
composed space
composed real
parabolic real

To which you often return
from which you never depart
—such is the rejoinder
delivered from elsewhere.

#

Delivered elsewhere
wrongly delivered
"delivery scheduled"
interrupted between worlds

Meaning the song
breaks into two
breaks
and breaks again

Meaning breaks
into mere number
evacuated regret
desire's hollowed core

Rounded into a sphere
rounded with a sleep
dissolved—
we are such stuff.

#

Resolved:
we are such stuff:
how could it be
among such absolutes?

The imperatives
the commands
the hectoring
voices

What is it
to listen
to instantly
obey?

This
(he said)
and
this.

#

Because the gestures
turn
one upon another
again and again

Because the figures
contain
a kind of clockwork
flywheels and gears

Because the sawdust
fills their skulls
packs itself
around their hearts

And the birds return
the badly stuffed vultures
monstrous and deaf
to my father's invocation.

##

Returning to the house
(prooftext or metatext)
returning to origins
always returning

Did we live here?
(here always an elsewhere)
was something spoken
over us in this place?

Were we brought to Justice
(foursquare, builded)
was everyone questioned
standing before the Law?

Only to be dismissed
(inevitable cycle)
only to depart
with a fond farewell.

\#

So that justice and love
are revealed to be the same
indistinguishable
in a grinding of wheels

Old-fashioned machinery
no microprocessors
here nothing
quite so instantaneous

Slow the accretion
steady the turns
the watchmen employed
forever employed

Or further back
hands upon the wheel
upon the strings the hands
and the voices rising.

#

The generative will
at peace with itself
in the voices rising
at peace with itself

It is in that place
that dialogue
that we
begin to understand

Begin
to make ourselves
and make ourselves
heard

For it
is an over-hearing
this overreaching:
listen.

#

Immense the enchantment
of this world
and
immense this world

Immense the disenchantment
of this world
over which contend
immense powers

Illusory powers
real but illusory
phantoms of our making
and not our making

I mean the magical
repetitions
the enchantment
and the disenchantment.

##

Why do I return
to certain figures
certain voices
always overheard?

If I were
and so
you would see that
and so

But no—
rather a stir
and stutter
rather a—

I mean the restlessness
the repression
I mean the reports
always coming in.

#

And the lyric? well,
birds, boats,
the elemental matters
elemental moments

See to their simplicity
always determined
incalculably determined:
"broils root out the work"

Oppose, oppose
with a twitch of the nerves
a breath of air
love's ephemera

As would make a song
wrest from chance
chant
the orders of the world.

#

These are the chanted
orders of the world
columns rising
no longer besmeared

These are the rising
figures of the world
one and one again
so that we may count

On them or with them
a simple measure
neither abandoned
nor triumphant

But counted:
I mean we
—it—
should count.

\#

A gift
an obligation
on both sides
an obligation

Responsive
responsible
under hand
under way

Arrived is to on the way
as never is to always
but to care for the passengers
for those who have booked passage

For those who
have chosen this passage
whatever the risks
the attendant pleasures.

##

"Only that it should be beautiful"
only that it should give pleasure
or as Joel inscribed it
(that night at the Omni—

12/7/79)—
"who gives beauty fully"
and in memory
of one lost

names, dates, & places:
so many they turn
back on themselves
coming to rest

3/23/01
the poem is dated
I hold the book in my hand
always at risk.

#

Beauty at risk
or beauty as risk
dubious pleasures
so late in the game

When you came that night
the world lost its mooring
found itself rebound
as we were held

As we held each other
broken, re-
paired:
the rest is commentary

The rest is a life
the rest of life
life as we live
now.

#

A track across the sky
extending from now
past the morning star
to the rest of life

The rest of the passage
the rest of the passengers
lost in the distance
too far to see

So that one can only
listen, listen—
"and he who listens hard
does not see"

But I would
see what I have seen again:
it would
suffice.

#

This must
suffice:
sufficient
unto the day

Unto that day
that horizon
the line beyond which
I cannot go

Or have gone already
see myself there
and you have to go
alone together

No guide or guidance
in desert or forest
or city street
and the roads beyond.

III

POWERS

When Pearse summoned Cuchulain to his side,
What stalked through the Post Office? What intellect,
What calculation, number, measurement, replied?
                —Yeats

So they loved as love in twain
Had the essence but in one,
Two distincts, division none:
Number there in love was slain.
                —Shakespeare

#

TRACK

##

This is the place
where strangeness ends

The place forever
folding in upon itself

Which those already
at home call home

And those without rest
can never know.

#

Came to that place
or were of that place

Had come to that place
so long ago

Had left that place
knowing that place

Something they carried
taking its place.

#

Something taking place
standing in place

Folded in place
and left standing

A moving place
never left behind

Wings folded
around that place.

#

Those without rest
knowing that place

Knowing where strangeness
begins and ends

Knowing they have left
and have never left

Knowing never
to speak of home.

##

As one who would gather
all things into presence

Gather all things
before they disappear

Would give them this charge:
gather unto yourself

All that is you
all that is here.

#

But all that was here
borne here from elsewhere?

All that was borne here
by the currents of time?

Walking against the currents
walking on the shore

Came into the presence
of what was here no longer.

#

A figure loved as fate
because we love only our fate

A presence imposed
against the presence of things

Against the present
imposed the future or the past

Something to love
from time to time.

#

So that we cannot embrace
the here and now

Cannot embrace
here and now

Who have loved the future like a mistress
—*said so long ago*

Could love freedom as a presence
freed of fate in time.

##

Wars
and forced migrations

Sojourns
and exiles

The numbers must be
taken into account

And the disfigurements
of the surfaces.

#

Hymn or
historiography?

Something of both
I imagine

Chronicle
born of chronicle

Wish
the Scholar/Translator were here.

#

Translation: you may no longer
write this way

Or: you may no longer
go this way

Those of you
awaiting translation

Right
this way.

#

The force of that order
enactment of that order

As if disfigured
hymns and chronicles

Translate
into a new order:

Meaning standing forth
standing against force.

##

Love of meaning stands forth
freed of fate in time

Went into the background
and returned emptyhanded

Returned empty
hands with nothing to hold

Mind with nothing to hold
or so it has been translated.

#

In the tractate
on the mastery of meaning

Recently delivered
and newly translated

The lovers of fate
came into the Presence

Standing
in an empty space.

#

But in the tractate
on the mastery of mastery

Came upon a scribe
in an empty space

Before an empty book
indistinguishable from the others

Lining the shelves
but still empty.

#

Read the sound as silence
past or present tense?

Read freedom as fate
who is giving these instructions?

Read translator as scribe
read consonants as vowels

Read constantly the vows

Untranslatable.

TRACK

##

The present set in italics
because of its urgency

The present set in italics
because it is ancillary

The present never
fully present

The present a formula
never set down.

#

The present a gift
gift of presence

Moment of beauty
moment of relief

Scintillant living
greens in the breeze

The sky the lawn
a moment here.

#

Walk into
that moment

Still a stranger
here at home?

Nothing more familiar
nothing more uncanny

(Ghosts) in the morning
guests at the door.

#

Guest   Ghost   Host
three figures with one face

Recall the text:
essay or film

Seen or read
so long ago

Three words with one root
at home so long ago.

##

So isolated
so connected

So isolated
because of the connections

The impalpable connections
ghosts in the machine

The little boy waiting
never growing up.

#

Waiting for rain
in a rainy season

Waiting for an earthquake
the existential shock

The shock of regularity
—*cut it in half!*

Break! cried the master
because the point

#

was not the point.

Because we are unhoused
because the litany

takes us up
takes us away

from or into
what is familiar

Because we are unbound.

#

Unbound, unhoused
alone or in families

The living and the dead
the real and the imagined

No choice but to obey

Neither eat the book
nor vomit it forth

One half falls away.

TRACK

            ##

So the lost tribes
find their way into the text

So the saving remnant
remains to be celebrated

Monad upon monad
each reflecting the other

Came upon the words
after endless repetition.

            #

Came upon the words
stolen as usual:

"A mode of assuring the seeker
that he is on the way

and is not merely wandering blindly
through the chaos from which

all form
rises."

#

The seeker here
was meant to be home

But is still on the way
despite our best intentions

Our best intentions?
—voice of god or fate?

Again that feeling
of wandering blindly.

#

"The chaos from which
all form rises"

"Wherefrom the shadows
that are forms fall"

Rising and falling
beyond any coincidence

That certainty before the text
which we can never reclaim

Honored Professor!

Your recently published memoirs, which have shocked and amazed even your most devoted students, are slowly revealing themselves to be a source of great inspiration for those who would continue your work. Yet much remains troubling. The conclusion that may be drawn from your observations regarding the ineluctable lateness of what we call the sacred now forces many of us to reexamine our most basic assumptions about the field. (I pass over the more personal implications of your remarks for those students who continue the attempt to reconcile their scholarly activities with the practice of an organized faith. Alas that we lack your own guidance here, since all evidence points to the probability that, prior to your departure, you destroyed the journal in which you kept your most intimate theological speculations.)

How have you convinced us of this lateness? What does it mean for the Rule of Primal Voices which you told us repeatedly was the guiding principle in your practice of translation? If I may borrow a line from one of your last completed renditions, "The world is made of his voice." Surely, master, many of us feel the same way about your work, and it is in precisely this conflation that the problem now lies.

"But paleography is not propaganda," you wrote, and the decisiveness of that assertion (it could stand as a motto for all your efforts) remains, a sharp contrast to the corrosive doubts poorly hidden in your other remarks. You noted early on that the scribes were also redactors. Does the same apply to the modern scholar/translator? You sensed that with your work, you had "become involved in the process of formation of the canon of this sacred material." Does the student of these archaic texts unveil or decode their sacred character, or in reality designate them, categorize them as sacred? You longed "to make available what I so wanted to keep secret and inviolable." Which, in the end, did you choose?

Esteemed sir, we have little choice but to carry on with these investigations, following your footsteps even into the most treacherous territory, the most ambiguous researches. Even the faith we place in what you called "the unsullied literary imagination," as evinced in these documents, is a faith in an ambiguous power, as fickle and unpredictable as the Yahweh of the later Hebrew scriptures. How remote and godlike becomes the precursor, how endlessly interpretable the founder of a discourse! And of whom do I speak when I lament the loss of that original author? You became the figure whom you sought. In turn you have become that figure for us. We know this by certain signs you have left. That have always been there.

Your devoted student,

TRACK

##

Layer upon layer
we return to the site
again and again
return to the sight

This was the origin
so long ago
the great island
and the outer boroughs

The romance of the streets
for the young archaeologist
is gone in the dust
of moments or years

Ash on the fruit
in the Amish Market
ash on the jars
ash in the jars.

#

Neither the sonnets
nor the clay tablets
the arc of fireworks
the haunted collage

Neither the impossibility
nor the incommensurability
—the proper tools
are always at hand

To free oneself
of sententious platitudes
music the ally
silence the ally

Turn to the task
turn the task
turn it
and turn it again.

#

The easy wisdom
the impossible ambiguities
gone in an instant
the complex of time

The constellation of phenomena
trajectory of forces
too complicated to calculate
too diffuse to predict

The stymied pundits
in the face of mourning
the threatened nation
gave him "strange courage"

Gave him hope
in the face of powers
powers beyond hope
powers of hope.

#

Sixteen is the number
he found on the card
too awful to picture
or to name

Awful the sense
of numbed fatality
out of the fatalities
in awful numbers

Only the flimsiest
game to guide him
so that he must ask pardon
—but of whom?

Himself or all of us
in the verbal reversals
setbacks, defeats
ruins upon ruins.

##

Not the mighty dead
with whom you are wont to wrestle
but the humble dead
who can swat you like a fly

There and there again
each morning in the Times
staring from sheets of newsprint
not from sheets of flame

What counts counts
in and beyond the poem
far beyond the poem
into empty space

Empty and full
full of emptiness
each morning in the Times
each morning in time.

#

Tell us the way
they sing without music
tell us of the shops
where they go to change

Colors, white to brown
or brown to white
tell us of how they eat
the food if it is frozen

Tell us if that is food
or a toy in the child's hand
or a room full of toys
or a shop full of toys

Tell us why the woman
walks so many dogs
tell us of the dogs please
before we have to go.

#

Tell us the news
that we want to know

Tells us the news
whether we want to know or not

Tells us
what it wants us to know

Whether we know it
or not

Whether it knows us
or not

Whether we know us
or not

What do we know?
only that we

Knowing that want
want to know.

#

Days such as these
the poet
seeks even more intently

for a language somehow commensurate
with the presentation of events
scarcely possible to follow.

Days such as these
the poet
can count on little that was not his

though from the beginning there was nothing
he could count
as his own.

Days such as these
the presentation of events
is owned and disowned continually

in the poet's search.

##

Lost and dreaming
among the antiquities
the dead world memorialized
if only in thought

He lived in a museum
at the edge of an abyss
lived in an abyss
resembling a museum

Shuffling through the corridors
invisible to the crowds
the invisible crowds
in what was really his home

The pots, the masks
the unidentified artifacts
that came from a time
before or after.

#

And he would hear things
now and then
not quite dictation
neither song nor speech

And he would see things
as if they were photographs
in the pages of a newspaper
he hadn't time to read

And he would know things
not really in advance
no more so than anyone
who cared to think about it

I mean he would be visited
by ancestors or descendents
would ascend or descend
without any choice.

#

I mean as time went on
there was little he could do
less and less
becoming more and more

Needs and demands
compounding the losses
the living continually
adding to the dead

Subtracting what he could keep
from what he believed he possessed
believing he was possessed
because all seemed lost

"All *is* lost": ashes, ashes
the memory of masters
masters of memory
lost and restored.

#

And when I love thee not
declared the great Captain
Chaos is come again
as chaos came again

How everything was falling
and knew it was true
for it was on a screen
for all to see

The philosopher
and the physicist
the critic and the missing
mathematician

All of them transformed
into connoisseurs of chaos
all gaping
at the loss of love.

##

But they provided a language
one of many
and that too
appeared upon a screen:

> Simple rules
> can build complex structures
> while maximizing functionality
> and minimizing resources

Or imagined it embroidered
upon a sampler
in an old-fashioned parlor
rocking chair and all

Repeated endlessly
part of a pattern
studied by intelligences
here and beyond.

#

From which perspective
little can be gained
so that one must return
to simple statements

Simple sentiments:
let's have it out:
*I believe in technique
as the test of a man's sincerity*

Wherefrom may follow
inevitable argument
unavoidable argument
and the music thereof

Say an idea
and its concomitant emotions
or an emotion
and its concomitant ideas.

#

Nor is this theory
or even poetics:
there is a hole in my city
as there is a hole in my heart

But the poet
has learned certain lessons
must have learned certain lessons
about weights and measures

Of words and their accuracy
prior to consolation
seeing, listening
reaching toward that goal

prooftext or metatext
here always an elsewhere
foursquare, builded
inevitable cycle

#

Therefore the repetition
of the text or act of love
leads inevitably
to the text or act of love

So that the consolation
appears to arise
out of a certain logic
built into the syntax

Built into the body
ears, eyes, genitals
posed against death
though "Deathward we ride"

So love calls to love
love calls for love
and the urgent master
calls love to task.

TRACK

##

*A place for prayer
or thought about prayer*

*Or thought about thought—
think of that!*

*Not quite a savage place
(holy and enchanted)*

*Adjacent or anterior
to a chamber now lost.*

#

*Or stanzas now lost?
(We'll build in sonnets pretty rooms)*

*Space for prayer
or space for writing?*

*As in a film
when the present dissolves*

*Rolls back as a curtain
and there you are.*

#

A place for love
(This bed thy center is,

these walls, thy sphere.)
—think of that!

Think of love
as that intelligent

That intelligence
guiding all.

#

Guiding the building
public and private

The merchants in the square
the lovers closeted

The scribes, the emissaries
waiting in the courtyard

Stargazers and masons
attending the debates.

##

Speaks of a garden
enclosed in a garden

A garden enclosed
within a translation.

A garden translated
from heaven to earth

A garden translated
from Greek to Hebrew.

#

Heaven?
earth?

Greek?
Hebrew?

Translation: a translation
or: a time

Crossing time
in time.

#

Therefore we cannot
fix this in time

Therefore we cannot
repair the time

Restore the time
translate the time

Make the time our own
make time.

#

Or unmake the time
unmake the boundaries
enclosing time

Unmake the translation
binding time
ruling time

Unmake the ruling
the rule of time.

##

Time of the gods
time of God

Unbounded time
before the rule of God

*Here the record
is broken and lost*

Here the record
is stolen and lost.

#

Stolen, lost
transformed, transgressed

The record of myth
the record as myth

The record a myth
after its disappearance

The record a myth
after its translation.

#

The myth a record
of translation or transgression

A scandal among the scribes
translating the myth

Recording the transgressions
of the schools and parties

*Here the record
is broken and lost.*

#

At some point the record
was spirited away

At some point the spirit
was taken away

Called forth, called away
summoned or stolen

Temple or archive

Loss of the prepositions.

##

These directions
to or from the archive
to or from the temple
cannot be reconstructed
cannot be translated
cannot be

Can teach us nothing
though the spirit lingers.

#

My father was a scribe
like his father before him

Enamored of the spirit
like his father before him

But the scriptures can teach us nothing
though the spirit lingers

In a place where we
may no longer go.

#

In a place where we
may no longer write

In a place about which
we may no longer write

Families of scribes
grown into tribes

Inspired
by an absent spirit.

#

Sign for "folded tent"
translated as "journey"

Signs for "sea," "tablet" and "wall"
translated as "archive"

Signs for "sky," "tablet" and "wall"
translated as "temple"

Sign for "journey"
translated as "scribe."

TRACK

##

Tribal inscription
or scribal instruction:

"to practice skill
in recording the force moving,

then to know it
in the largeness of its proportions—"

Then to take it
to heart.

#

Then to take it
away on a journey

To practice the skill
while sojourning among strangers

Dreaming inscriptions
inscribing dreams

Waiting
for the next word.

#

Listening
for the next word

So that everything
comes to signify

Points backward
points forward

Until we are led
to choose.

#

Even now
after so long

I cannot comfort
myself with such choices

As I have long sought
to comfort others

Daring language
daring the precinct.

##

Rest here
though it is still moving

Though they are still moving
toward or away from home

Rest here
in what may become a precinct

Because you are here
because you have chosen.

#

Because you have chosen
you have been chosen

Translator, scribe
hermeneutical apostate

Disciple of the god
in the service of God

Pressed into service
somewhere along the way.

#

Pressed into service—
the perpetual motif

How it is written
why it is written

What comes to be written
again and again

Until the motif
becomes the motive

#

In these operations
no single motif

*In these inscriptions
no single motive*

*Despite the claims
no single motive*

Despite the claims
now and then.

TRACK

##

The indistinguishable voices
haunting the precinct

Holy or unholy
wholly indistinguishable

Has led us to conflate
time with time

Precinct with precinct
voices with silence.

#

So that listening
to an act of reverence

Becomes an act of reverence
hovering in translation

The scribes and redactors
become scribes and redactors

Enacting the losses
lost in translation.

#

Gathering, arranging
the endless repetitions

At risk of ending
at any moment

Any moment suffused
with ending or beginning

"*Now* that tremendous
plunge"

#

Any moment suffused
with endless quotation

Quotation as translation
beyond all strategies

Lifting the text
in and out of time

"these certainties against
the all-uncertain"

Dear T,

In the context of this project, nothing is more ironic than prose. A letter, a report, a commentary, a meditation: prose immediately suggests a second-order discourse that cannot be translated back into an original, even when the original appears to consist mainly of repetition and quotation. So why write to you in this predictable and probably ineffective fashion? Is it only a matter of completing the structure ordained in advance?

Almost, but not quite. Prose has the virtue of clarity, a virtue that is by no means innate, but is actually bestowed upon it by the expectations of its readers. The pressure of that expectation has been traditionally welcomed by some of the greatest practitioners, who have produced key texts—texts that have opened previously locked doors—when they have been most conscious of their readers' needs.

Does there seem to be a contradiction here? Does the irony I observed negate the clarity that is so desired? I can think of one instance in the scribal history in which the most open invitation to interpretation resulted in the most strenuous resistance to stable meaning. The expectation of clarity in that instance led to the most uncanny of linguistic deferments and frustrating of paradoxes. And yet each word seemed a mirror of the reader's thoughts.

No, one cannot assume that these are contradictory circumstances. I can think of occasions—certainly disastrous, even cataclysmic, but those too of less extreme rupture in the pattern of life—in which one is compelled, obligated to speak with the utmost precision, and may yet be held back for the very same reasons. Then language can manifest itself only in this double nature.

Such being the case, sometimes we have no choice but to write these letters—these reports, commentaries, meditations. And I write this knowing you are gone, knowing that at best, I write to, into, from, the path you may have taken. I am dismayed by neither the derivative nature of the task nor by its ultimate futility. Which is not to say that I don't believe you will get the message.

Love always,

##

TRACK

##

All spells recalled
but still accountable

Lost glamour, lost grammar
but still accountable

Lost gramarye.

#

Lost grimoire:

Soul-eater possibly
put to rest

Or never put to rest
now that all is lost.

#

"Only the faithful
hold this place green"

The magic withdrawn
the book dismembered

And the blessings and curses of the Lord.

#

Gone in an instant
gone into the dance

Gone into the abyss
the wizard and his foe

All power drained away.

#

Sexual potency
replacing the spells

Replacing the names

Soul and soul-eater
yielding to the flesh.

##

They were invested
in that magic

So was I

They were invested
in that language.

#

Was there any choice?

Yes, the world answered:
here is pain and beauty
in equal measure

Equal to any magic.

#

Or another order
of the same magic?

Here at the cabin
chipmunks, chickadees

So close to hand.

#

So close one can only
react with pleasure

The dis-ease of pleasure
pleasure of dis-ease

The jay squawking in the aspens.

#

The jay squawking
asking for more

More magic
in the simplicity of its hunger

Than the poem can sustain.

##

And yet the poem
must sustain all things

All of the orders
as have been prescribed

As have been ordered.

#

Therefore and
therefore

Not that it can be explained
not that it can be inscribed

But still.

#

Nor is language magic
as in some cabal
waving their wands

Not magic but mystery
into which one may go.

#

Into which one may go
when one's name is called

Called by the Name
the nameless Name

Called into the nameless.

#

Not mystification
but a simple mystery

The self and the world
are made manifest in language

Called out of the nameless.

But why am I called
to use *this* language?

So wise, she said
putting me ill at ease
troubling the waters.

Doubling the sense:

Brooding over the waters
or burning in the abyss

What should and should not be

What I know and do not know.

What I know
is that one is called

What I do not know
is the caller

If that matters.

#

What I know is that
in idleness or urgency

The call descends
the response ascends

That is the matter.

#

One finds oneself
in such a place

Or one finds that one
has been put in a place

Holy and enchanted.

##

Circular place
circular tower
circular ruins

Ruins of a circle
frequently empty.

\#

Woven thrice
but still empty

Still vacant
as if an occupant
could be found.

\#

As if a practice
could be founded

Risky business
for those who know

But worth the investment.

#

Our founder
thrice blessed

At the circle's center
thrice woven

A portrait on the wall.

#

Admirable
but unacceptable

An unacceptable offer

These risks
these returns.

TRACK
(site of the author)

I sought a form
Spoken to me
More than any metaphor
Subject or subjectless
There in the desert
There at the mountain
I could not disagree
A pure synecdoche
This mineral being
Universally applied

And so descended
Or rose out of Chaos
Event or progress
No source of ethics
No model of behavior
No model of form
So that finding
Reason of reason
Becomes what we have

The urgency to build
Form out of the formless
An uncut altar
Between nature and culture
Body and building
Struck by the spirit
Poured from every orifice
Temples and stars

Fortunate and unfortunate
Departure unto departure
Too many to count
Would list them for you
Construct a collage
Lobsters and butterflies
For a pedlar become a queen

Wyrm Queen or Ice Queen
Dressed in a pinafore
At a table in the passageway
The rebbe's table
Expounding the seduction
Here and among the stars

Five or six points
Remains to be determined
Necromancy or prophecy
To whom am I speaking?
How long have I slept?

Departed long ago
This is my letter
This is not my letter
Departed but never arrived

Never learning to listen
Never learning to see
Never learning to count

Matter out of repetition
Power out of repetition

IS IT NOT IT IS

Framed so at the center
Forever becoming law

Until a tower controlled the sky
The quotations become a politics
The politics nothing but quotations

The reversals nothing but politics
Accused and judged guilty
Guilt born out of innocence
Experience perpetually reborn

When I first came to this country
Errour had been slayne
Knights and ladies would appear
Transformations grew unbearable
Swords beaten into books

Now I must listen carefully
Five or six lines
Swords or stars in a well
Sight fell in and drowned
Speech fell in and drowned
This became the music

Album leaf or oak leaf
Found along the path
She lost her gentility
Ferocious docility
Her filigreed scissors
Cats and maidens
Salamanders and moths

Tell them I am not coming home
Regardless of any regrets
Tell them the house was never mine
Tell them they can have it
Furniture and incoherence
The music so soothing
In the shadows of the maples
And the squadrons overhead

Walking out of the newspapers
An impossible peace
You used to add a yellow powder
As history accelerated
They used to walk beneath the maples
Before the system reached warp speed
But in the photograph they are seated
Both dressed in pea jackets
As if the past were a refrain

To play this music
You cannot love this music
Too much or too little
On this or any flight
That is the law
The police have arrived
I cannot say if they are heroes
Their shields are tablets
They wait for the sign
This is the sign

TRACK

##

Bob and Cindy
never made it home

The kids were found wandering
near the abandoned minivan:

Pop culture.

#

Pop quiz:

Is the music on the CD
that you play in the car

The soundtrack to a movie
that becomes your life?

#

Dear Steve,

Enclosed are the instructions
which I trust you'll follow.

Love,
    Pop

#

Dear Dad,

Ever since I moved here,
people call me Norm
without thinking twice.

Can I come home please?

#

Dear Norm,

We never liked scrabble,
you sonuvabitch.
Now look at us.

Bob and Cindy

##

After the internal
censors are laid to rest

After the carnival
has packed up and left

There are only the numbers.

#

There are only the names
and the reports of the names

The stolen names
the names in disguise

Your name and mine.

#

Dear A, How is it
that after all this time

You are a letter in a letter
a name in a rhyme?

Love,

#

Who?

"N" or "The Author"
I suppose

"I" or "The Author"
we suppose.

#

We suppose the numbers
determine the names

Or the names
determine the numbers

Here and there.

##

Perhaps there is
no here and there

No adverbial
or pronomial shifts

No names or places.

\#

Meaning no beyond
no other

Portentous claptrap
out of which "we" construct

Certain powers.

\#

No games
after all the games

Stripping or baring
—not that game either

But how to load and bless.

#

And I think of another
recently gone

Coming in his youth
to "the last defense"

Freed of all quotation.

#

The instant becomes elegy

Read this beyond the line

Read this past all markers

Read this as "our" score

"Our" struggle.

##

So word by word, and line by line
    The dead man touched me from the past,
    And all at once it seemed at last
The living soul was flashed on mine

Guest   Ghost   Host

#

But suppose then
that the house is empty

Not haunted but empty
so that all is elegy

Zero or negative numbers.

#

How to represent that?
how to give it form?

Suppose then
that before the zero
lies a counter-track.

#

Suppose then
that the elegy moves
before the loss

The matter of the poem
its anti-matter.

#

Not the uncanny
but the canny

Not the unhoused
but a dark house

Behold me,

##

*for I cannot sleep
and like a guilty thing I creep
At the earliest morning to the door.*

Overrunning the boundaries
to speak of it.

#

Overrunning the boundaries
the bounding line
to which we must hold

Though it may be an illusion
still it must hold.

#

Except for those moments
when art cannot hold

When from over the line
that art cannot hold

Come the messages.

#

Come the messengers
whose presence is the message
that the boundaries have dissolved

Whose presence announces
that you may cross the line.

#

Between the living and the dead
the past and the present

The dead make a present
of their future presence

In and out of time.

TRACK

##

When you fall down the well
or look into the mirror

A basin of water
drawn from that well

There are five or six stars
or swords glinting in starlight.

#

There are five or six stars
made out of swords

There are five or six lines
inscribed on the swords

There are five or six doors
to five or six powers.

#

So that you see yourself walking
there among the ruins

The broken porticoes
pediments become impediments

Sharp as swords
before five or six doorways.

#

So that the way is blocked
—do you remember?

I see a boy and his mother
I see a boy and his father
I see them reading together

This is the first impediment.

#

I see the boy and his mother
hurrying through the crowd

I see the father in his chair
I see an empty chair

I don't remember anything

The door shuts behind you.

#

Doors	Stars	Water
Powers	Swords	Mirror

##

In which you see
people coming toward you
or turning away

Reaching toward them
or turning away

This is the second impediment.

#

Or a letter arrives
from one believed lost

Or a visitor arrives
whom you cannot bear to see

He demands you come downstairs
so down you go.

#

From the bedroom upstairs
where you dress in white

With the goblin lover
mouldering playmate

Waking together
waking alone.

#

Could that be the love
from which you must turn?

Turn down the covers
of a bed of stone?

Walk among stones
until love has died?

#

For you must go alone
out of starry midnight

You must go alone
past the morning star

Perhaps love will reach you
perhaps not.

#

Neither man nor woman
(cast your white dress away)

Neither lover nor beloved
(the morning rises around you)

The door shuts behind you

The crowd is cheering.

##

Standing on the balcony
of the presidential palace

Or seated in the studio
reading comics and poems

The crowd longs to hear you
to see you in the flesh.

#

The disembodied flesh
the face on the airwaves

Face on the screen
so wise and secure

Who would have believed it?

This is the third impediment.

#

Either they know everything
or they know nothing

So you have been told

Either you know everything
or you know nothing

So they have been told.

#

Either the crowd
is out there for the hell of it

Or for an unfathomable purpose
that may yet unfold

That may yet be understood
if we are given the time.

#

If we take the time
seize the time

Risk the time
whether we may or not

Time and again
losing time.

#

Time of the now
or ruins of time

No angel of history
hovering above the crowd

No guardian or doorkeeper

The door shuts behind you.

[##]

In this place I would have spoken
to You or of You

In this place I would have left
all else behind

What do I have
in place of this place?

[#]

This is the fourth impediment
—but it is no impediment at all!

There is nothing under foot
nothing in the way

No track at all
leading to no power.

[#]

Which is its power
and has been all along

I mean what has been
all along the way

I mean what You mean
all along the way.

[#]

I mean in Your power
You sent me on my way

I mean without Your power
I was sent on my way

Powerless
I went my way.

[#]

Except I had a power
the power of the way

Neither on the way
to You or from You

On my own way

This is *the fourth impediment!*

[#]

Come out from this place
that is no place

Here there is nothing
that can take its place

And no door to
or from this place.

##

Came from the moon
landed in front of him
there on the way

Stepped from a spaceship
resembling a minivan
armed with arrows and a bow.

#

Stepped from a chariot
surrounded by hounds
with arms long and small

Huntress, hunted
chased or fleeing
—the lunar dance.

#

This is the fifth impediment
not quite as intended
but still unreal

Language was to be
the fifth impediment:
fictions.

#

Cursed with strong
imaginations
they lay themselves down
beneath the moon

In broad daylight
but beneath the moon.

#

Took comfort in the fact
that he was dreaming

Took comfort in the fact
that she could kiss him at will

Took comfort
in a thing of beauty.

#

"The key turns,
and the door upon its hinges groans."

Slipping away
through one door or another

Hand in hand
in the moonlight.

##

Well, they are gone
and this nears an end:
this is the last impediment

Yes, the thing itself
with which we cannot dispense:
cold pastoral.

#

Yes, they are gone
and I am left alone

Alone with the alphabet
and all of the figures

Here in this bower
here in this cell.

#

Here in this cell
I have written a mystagogy
though it was not my intention

To do or to love
a thing too much
—for which I beg forgiveness.

#

The Author begs forgiveness
of all from whom he stole

Initials, identities,
imaginary figurations

Like so many love letters
I give them back.

#

I give them back
and walk through the door

I shut it behind me
and toss away the key

The house disappears
and the road too.

#

In the gray space
where the ghosts gather

In mist or in flame
calling and calling

I give up the book
and take myself back.

##

Came with broken hearts
came from all points of the compass rose
or compass star
5x5
6x6
7x7

Came to a bridge.

#

Crossed the bridge
into the city

Held each other
upon the bridge

Kissed
with the city all before them

Took their picture.

#

Coming from wherever
this foreign couple

Tourists or immigrants
with hardly any English

Hardly any experience
but a walk upon the bridge

2 or 3x1.

#

Nothing climactic
but a casual promise
in all its power

A stroll across the bridge
some years hence

5x2
2x1.

#

Or to see myself writing
a book in a room

On an island where I lived once
as an innocent child

On an island where I never
lost my innocence

1x1 or 1x2.

#

So that I come
into a strange company:

"more to me,
and more in my meditations,
than you might suppose."

Giving or taking up
all of the names.

#

Weeping for sorrow
weeping for joy

There on the bridge
camera in hand

There in a room
I will never   see?

Namaste   הנני

Statements for *Track*

The following passages, taken from my notebooks, were written while I was working on *Columns* and *Powers*. I am grateful to Peter O'Leary, who convinced me that they might be of interest. I hope that Peter is right.

##

10/7/99

Track is a series of controlled discontinuities, the self-conscious dilapidation of the structuralist's dream as it ascends toward the transcendental signifier. The poem as "field of action" or "park of eternal events" applies to my work only insofar as the action or events can be both determined *and* left open to happenstance. Linguistic and experiential pressures brought to bear on the writing (and again, this is a matter of deliberation *and* accident) set off "articulations of sound forms in time," or lyric moments arising in spite of themselves. *Track* is the lyric of disaster, the disaster of lyric. It inoculates itself through measured sequences of verbal shocks, which then reveal themselves as parts of a larger pattern. It becomes a totality in spite of itself, and it is under this condition that it continues to be conceived and composed. Always at odds with itself, it requires a grandiosity that must be continually punctured, sufficiently punctured in an act that is still a shaping, still formal. Its place in the course of my work in general is thus inevitable and extreme.

#

12/25/99

Another way to look at it: *Track* is the result of the conjunction of (or the tension between) a (post-) Objectivist procedure and a sensibility that is personal, perhaps even confessional, devotional, religious. None of these terms are as precise as I'd like; it could be that I can't be more exact than this, however. There's even less point in cataloguing influences. If *Track* keeps leading back and around—obsessively—to certain sites, it is because repetition in itself is a kind of epiphany. What does one hear, what does one see? How does that play out, how is it constituted, in a particular, rarefied universe of discourse? Why, and how, does it bend backward into the self? At what points, under what rhetorical conditions, is that self dissolved, and at what points, conversely, is it reconstituted? And why, above all, is this a matter of numbers, and the level of abstraction they represent?

#

10/8/00

The small, odd moments in *Track*, often more visual than aural, continue to intrigue me. They *don't* always signify the breaking in of Discontinuity as Presence, which remains crucial to the work, but I don't necessarily see them as gimmicks or novelties or mere embellishments either. What we like, or what can take us furthest (sometimes the same thing, sometimes not), does not, as Adam Phillips writes, "always accord with our standards." In the chapter "Sexes" in *Terrors and Experts*, Phillips observes the following, which I like so much that I'll copy it out, thinking that "poetry" could replace "psychoanalysis" at certain points, and that "poetic" could replace "erotic":

> Most psychoanalytic theory now is a contemporary version of the etiquette book; improving our internal manners, advising us on our best sexual behaviour (usually called maturity, or mental health, or a decentered self). It is, indeed, dismaying how quickly psychoanalysis has become the science of the sensible passions, as though the aim of psychoanalysis was to make people more intelligible to themselves rather than to realize how strange they are. When psychoanalysis makes too much sense, or makes sense of too much, it turns into exactly the symptom it is trying to cure: defensive knowingness. But there is nothing like sexuality, of course, for making a mockery of our self-knowledge. In our erotic lives, at least, our preferences do not always accord with our standards. We are excited by the oddest things, and sometimes people.

Poetry, of course, does not seek to cure anything, though what Phillips calls "defensive knowingness" can be as much a problem in the world of poetry as it can in the realm of human behavior. And there is no question that there are times when poetry makes too much sense or makes sense of too much. This has nothing to do with what is usually understood as style: Charles Bernstein's poetry, for instance, falls prey to this as much as, say, Anthony Hecht's. Poetry that seeks to make itself intelligible to itself—a poetry of (self-) knowledge—runs a great risk. An overt instance of this (though recently I think the instances are more subtle and varied) was the Olson/Duncan conflict as seen in 'Against Wisdom As Such.'
But what about poetry that seeks to realize its strangeness to itself? *Track*, to a certain extent, is that kind of poetry. Just a year ago, I see, I spoke of

the poem as a "series of controlled discontinuities," which is precisely a making manifest or a realizing of strangeness. The incursion of a certain kind of pleasure/terror, akin to the strong incursions of eros into one's life, is registered through a shift in the verbal patterning, until it potentially becomes a part of the patterning. Appropriately, Phillips has a chapter ("Dreams"), in which he tropes on Kafka's parable of the leopards in the temple. The question is: what does it take to reveal that strangeness?; or, how do we know, and signify, that strangeness has come? Incursions into the poem of the sort I mean are almost by definition uncanny, whether experienced on the level of the visual or aural text, or both.

#

10/9/00

But what exactly is the nature of these uncanny incursions? What freight do they carry? Henry [Weinfield], responding to the material from Vol. 2 that I gave him recently, says that "I want Norman to be *there* more than you want to be. You're still sometimes flirting with a disembodied poetics, the poetic of language poetry, but you're just as much a humanist as you say I am." He goes on to speak of "a poetry that both cedes the initiative to words and yet is committed to *being here*." I responded by saying that in *Track*, I am trying to deconstruct the binary opposition between a (humanist?) poetry of presence and a (postmodern?) poetry of rupture, absence, etc. Thus, it would seem to me that the incursions of which I speak may appear as either postmodern gestures *or* expressions of "Norman" being there. Procedure or pattern, deduced, for the most part, arithmetically, is a set-up. But it's also, undeniably, the structure, and structure is still what it's all about. Why? Because what we "loveth best" reveals itself (sometimes coming from an outside, a scary event) only against or through or coming suddenly into the structure. So, indeed, the uncanny is heimlich in its unheimlich nature, insofar as it reveals itself as the best (and therefore first) beloved.

#

1/27/01

How to end the second volume, to say nothing of the poem as a whole? The last movement seems transitional, though I'm pleased with it. The idea of address didn't go quite where I expected it, though in a typical *Track* trajectory, it turned on itself, encompassed some repetition (or entered into a previously seen dimension) and then went "outward" (or at least gestured that way). The "numerology" continues to be slightly skewed—again, not a problem. In the light of what's gone on so far in ##, I'm reminded of Kafka's parable 'On Parables': "When the sage says: 'Go over', he does not mean that we should cross to some actual place, which we could do anyhow if the labor were worth it; he means some fabulous yonder, something unknown to us, something that he cannot designate more precisely either, and therefore cannot help us here in the very least." And as we know, it gets worse: "But the cares we have to struggle with every day: that is a different matter." Indeed.

If the labor were worth it—neither an actual place nor a fabulous yonder, and yet in this poem, I find myself "going over" willy-nilly. It is as if (ah!) the poem is always creating a potential within itself, a fold in the real (the composed). Hell opens to receive the fallen angels and in doing so, becomes that place. Or Satan lands, and in that crash landing hell opens up around him. But the space here is not hell, in any conventional sense, though it may be related to the mind's own place. Between the actual and the fabulous (Kansas is not the real and Oz is not the fabulous, contrary to popular belief), there is, for lack of a better term, a parabolic reality, and its fundamental quality is order, the composed—form and the breaking of form both. In a certain respect, we can say that the poem is always in *and* journeying toward a Promised Land. So I ask again, even presuming I've just learned something (doubtful): how does it end?

#

1/29/01

Further question: would it end when it so fully repeats itself that it's clear the serpent has its tail in its mouth? I hope not: the degree of predictability there would be disappointing and uninteresting, to say the least. An exhaustion of invention. No, better to acknowledge its interminability and simply cut it off at some point, abandoning it in the truest sense of Valéry's remark. But that too has its problems, which are the opposite of those that arise (triumphalism) in seeking some grand finale. The answer lies *elsewhere*—and not, I think, somewhere even between the poles I just described. For how does one represent an elsewhere? Don't ask the author of *The Utopian Moment*. Don't even try to find him—he's long gone.

#

8/1/01

Part of the problem of being a "poet/critic" lies in the heightened awareness and concomitant self-consciousness of the current "issues" or "conditions" in the "production" of new poetry. The quotation marks say it all. Not only is beauty difficult but irony is difficult as well, for it devolves too often into a corrosive attitude, a sour stomach, a jaded perspective. Yet we crave the new: that which may well emerge from the circumstances we can describe, but which nevertheless open the door to an elsewhere that is and is not strange and familiar. And this itself is an old story.

Just today, maybe yesterday, I was reading somewhere about the value of repetition. Not in the Kierkegaardian sense, but more along the lines of Augustine—that it tells us we're at least going somewhere. Here is Augustine: "A mode of assuring the seeker that he is on the way and is not merely wandering blindly through the chaos from which all form rises." Odd but true. If *Track* is a grand set of loops or repetitive fractals, then process will take precedence, and we are faced with the sort of formalism I've always found rather dubious. My skepticism in the face of my own methodology could stop me dead. Does poetry only tell us what we already know? What we want to hear? Even when we're discomfited, uneasy? Partly it's a matter of what Bronk, Williams, Weinfield speak of—the poem buried beneath the language, the certainty in the all-uncertain, the desert music. Well and good. One finds then, when all is working, the same familiar tune. Or a prize one wrests from chaos, noise, formlessness. Is that why you returned so long ago to the order of numbers? That sureness . . .

I don't know. At times I seem to falter so easily; I put my foot in my mouth; I'm so dumb. Not even, as I said at the outset of the poem, too smart for my own good. Just a schlemiel or worse in every dimension. Oh, I know I'm not. But to be competent, confident, have a few folks in life or poetry to rely on me, and to come through for them. Fine. And to be patient and do your work. Fine. ———

Several minutes go by. Dissatisfaction. *Track* is neither autobiographical grousing, linguistic game, nor cultural pronouncement. It is not the voice of the self, the voice of the other, the voice of a ghost, the voice of language. No, none of the above. It is not a grand refusal, but it's not a gracious acceptance of the world's invitation either. Ladies and gentlemen of the jury, I don't know why I started it and I don't know why I stay with it. Nor, for that matter, why "it" stays with me. If it does.

#

2/19/02

The trajectory of the final volume—an approach to or attempt to establish a home, a pleroma, which is a resting place in all senses of the term, which is also an uncovering or excavation of what had been such—thus simultaneously anticipatory and retrospective. Then broken, ruptured by the immediate, the exigency of the present, in a movement that is a work of mourning and an attempt to get one's bearings, in the end folding back, returning "to the text or act of love."

In previous volumes, some sort of form—formal marker—would continue to break/continue—continue to break—break to continue. The principle of repetition would demand this again, but also would be contented if another instance or type of repetition were to occur instead. But what? *Track* vacillates between a hypostatizing discourse and an indirectly personal discourse, though neither of these terms, strictly speaking, is accurate. As for looking forward to an "ending," "closure" is and is not desirable, is and is not possible. This is not, after all, Dante, but neither is it Duncan. Closer, I guess, to Zukofsky or Johnson but substance and form are still different enough. "I" will come to a number or a number will come to "me." Which is to say a form, bearing, I suppose, its content, will make itself manifest. It should call, which may be right where we are currently. As usual, we have been here before.

(NO) Message from the throne.

#

3/12/02

Preparing for my presentation at ASU. Rereading Joe Conte's *Unending Design*, which I continue to admire immensely. His typology remains very helpful in thinking about *Track*. <u>In most respects</u>, the work conforms to his definition of the serial poem of the "infinite" variety, despite the fact that I would like to bring it to a definite end. This leads to certain issues . . . —oh well, maybe, since he correlates Spicer's haunted house to the "finite" series, p'raps *Track* is more that sort of text. One can drive oneself crazy with this stuff, though the poem is certainly serial <u>in most respects</u>. Except that the numerology operative within each movement relates it to procedural forms too—one sets an arbitrary, predetermined rule or rules. Anyway, Conte says, thinking first of Creeley's *Pieces*, that discontinuity in the series "disrupts any internal development or progression of its materials. The sections of a series are not hierarchical. There is not initiation, climax or terminus precisely because there can be no development. In the sequence, the reader must, so to speak, enter through the front door and exit through the rear; but in a series such as Robert Duncan's *Passages*, the reader is encouraged to select any of these 'passages' as an entrance. The reader does not require the information of any one section in order to comprehend the others."

So how true is this of my work-in-progress? I guess I would accept most of the above statements as applicable. A reader could begin anywhere, though in later sections, he wouldn't be aware of the repetition from earlier ones. I'll say there's no hierarchy, but I'm not prepared to say yea or nay in regard to development, because there can be all sorts of development, both formal and thematic, and I might not (maybe best not) be aware of them all. One can only be one's own critic to some extent, and not too much at all is best. The degree of "hybridization" amongst these postmodern forms is very great. The form presents itself, and continues to do so. The proceduralism was always intended to be disrupted, though intentional disruptions were also subject to dictation, chance, etc. The tension between the predetermined and the aleatory remains strong, at least as I experience it, however it ends up looking.

#

5/29/02

The "division material" repeats itself *forward*, not *backward*, which doesn't make it symmetrical as fanning forward and backward from the center (the 16ers). So that's how the big # of *Powers* goes (is going, will go).

But—this machine—these concerns—is it a system-monster that eats everything as it marches toward some endless horizon, beyond which is some cloudy Absolute? A Kafkan fate, which one can imagine abandoning, as K his novels. With pleasure or regret? Shame? To love the ordinary up to the limits of (one's) language. To love invention, even if it feels derivative.

"All that's left is pattern* (shoes?)"

To understand that the shocks are to be expected, are and are not shocks. And that this makes it beautiful.

www.ingramcontent.com/pod-product-compliance
Lightning Source LLC
Chambersburg PA
CBHW022001160426
43197CB00007B/226